everything
a girl needs to know
about her

periods

everything a girl needs to know about her

periods

RONNIE
SELLERS
PRODUCTIONS
PORTLAND, MAINE

contents

how to use this book   6

section one: body basics
you have your first period when…   8
the first period—the signals   10
the first period—more signals   12
why you have a period   14
what starts my periods?   16
the two big hormones   18
from childhood to puberty:
    the outer signs   20
from childhood to puberty:
    the inside story   22
from childhood to puberty:
    more on the inside story   24
periods are good for you   26
your first period   28

section two: day-by-day

the whole month day-by-day	30
days 1&2	32
days 3&4	38
days 5 to 7	44
days 8&9	50
days 10 to 12	56
days 13&14	62
days 15&16	68
days 17 to 20	74
days 21&22	80
days 23&24	86
days 25&26	96
days 27&28	104
keeping a record	112

section three: help!

help! answers to your questions	116
how many periods will I have?	118
my periods aren't regular	119
what if I don't have a period?	120
my periods are too heavy	122
what should I wear— a tampon or a pad?	124
how do I use a pad?	126
how do I use a tampon?	128
what can I do to relieve cramps?	130
what should I eat?	132
what if I'm a vegetarian?	134
food chart	136
what's an internal exam?	138
words, words, words, a glossary	140
index	142

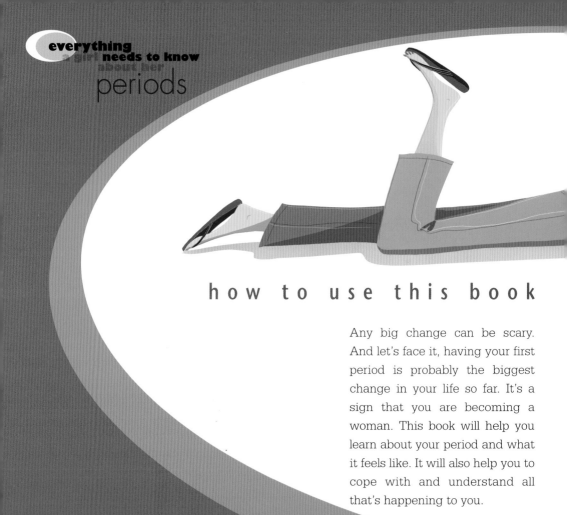

how to use this book

Any big change can be scary. And let's face it, having your first period is probably the biggest change in your life so far. It's a sign that you are becoming a woman. This book will help you learn about your period and what it feels like. It will also help you to cope with and understand all that's happening to you.

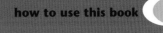

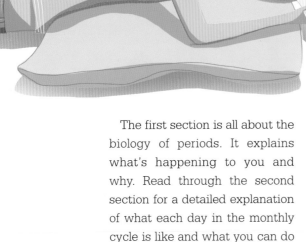

The first section is all about the biology of periods. It explains what's happening to you and why. Read through the second section for a detailed explanation of what each day in the monthly cycle is like and what you can do to feel your best.

The third section provides answers to questions you may have about periods. Remember, the more you know about the menstrual cycle, the better equipped you will be to deal with your own period.

Knowing what to expect will help you feel more in control. When you're in control, you're less anxious, and better able to enjoy life.

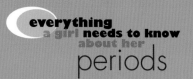

everything
a girl needs to know
about her
periods

1 you have your first period when...

your body's good and ready. You can't make your period start and you certainly can't stop it from coming. Your period will occur whether or not you understand what's happening in your body. But you are much more likely to feel better if you know what to expect.

The next section of the book will describe what's going on inside of you during each phase of the cycle. Remember, knowing these things about yourself will enable you to feel in control, and feeling in control is the key to feeling good.

everything
a girl needs to know
about her
periods

the first period—the signals

It's impossible to say exactly when you'll start your first period. But your body sends signals to tell you that you're likely to start soon.

Puberty is the time that your body develops sexually. This process begins between the ages of 8 and 15. Periods are a part of puberty, but they don't usually start until you are well on the way to changing from a child into a woman. Once puberty begins, it can take between six months and three years for your first period to occur. Usually, periods start between 18 and 24 months after your breasts begin

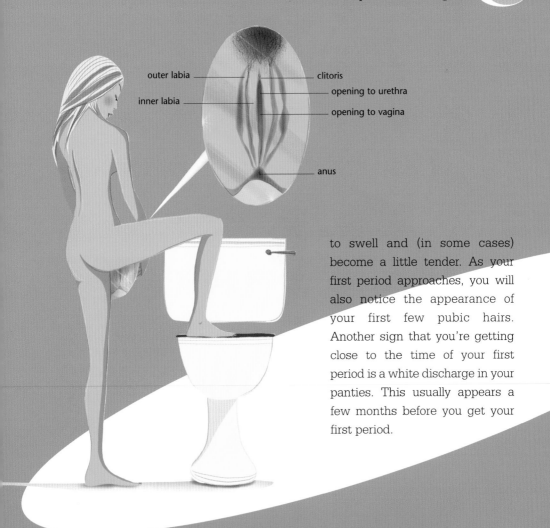

outer labia

inner labia

clitoris

opening to urethra

opening to vagina

anus

to swell and (in some cases) become a little tender. As your first period approaches, you will also notice the appearance of your first few pubic hairs. Another sign that you're getting close to the time of your first period is a white discharge in your panties. This usually appears a few months before you get your first period.

the first period—more signals

Finding a red-brown stain in your panties or on the sheets when you wake up in the morning might be the only sign that your period has started for the first time. That's the way it is for lots of girls. But you may also be able to tell that your period is about to start by the way you feel.

During the week before your period, you may be more emotional than usual. Your parents and friends may find you more irritable or moody, although you might simply feel more sensitive to whatever's happening. Some girls find that zits pop out just before their period. Others may have an ache or cramps in the lower part of their tummy. These cramps are not serious and you can often just ignore them. All these signs that occur just before a woman's period are called "premenstrual symptoms."

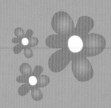

everything
a girl needs to know about her
periods

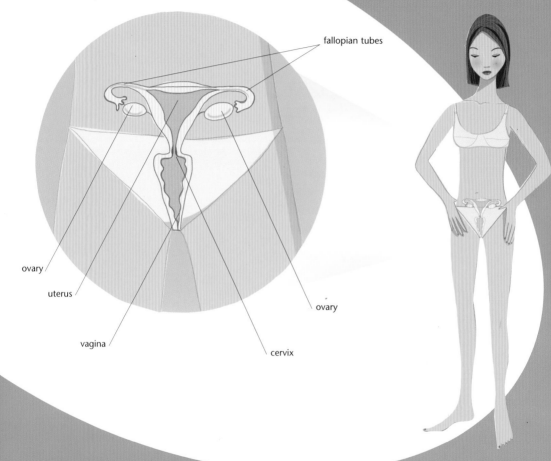

fallopian tubes

ovary

uterus

vagina

cervix

ovary

why you have a period

You were born with two ovaries, each of which came with a lifetime supply of thousands of tiny eggs. From the time you reach puberty until menopause, your ovaries release one of those eggs around the midpoint of every menstrual cycle. This is called ovulation.

Your body gets ready for the egg by creating a lining in the womb. This lining, made of tissue, fills with blood and nutrients that could feed a baby.

The ripe egg travels down the fallopian tubes into the womb. If a sperm has been deposited in the womb by a male, it may fertilize the egg. If that occurs, then a baby will grow in the womb.

If the egg is not fertilized, the body flushes it out along with with the blood, mucus, and tissue of the unused lining. During your period, this material flows from the womb through the cervix and out through the vagina.

> Only about half of the menstrual flow is actually blood. The rest is the spongy lining of the womb and mucus.

what starts my periods?

The short answer is hormones. These natural chemicals travel in the bloodstream and act as "messengers" in your body. Some hormones control the way your body grows. Others keep all the organs working properly. The special hormones that control puberty are called sex hormones. The same hormones exist in boys and girls, but they affect males and females differently. You may be surprised to learn that menstruation begins in your brain. When your body reaches a certain stage, your brain releases a hormone called gonadotropin-releasing hormone (GnRH for short). This marks the beginning of puberty. GnRH signals the pituitary gland, located at the base of your brain, to produce two sex hormones. These are called luteinizing hormone (LH) and follicle-stimulating hormone (FSH). Every month, these two hormones travel to the ovaries. FSH starts the development of the egg. Once the egg is ripe, LH triggers ovulation.

The hormones FSH and LH act on the ovaries to produce estrogen, the most important female sex hormone. Estrogen produces the changes that begin with puberty. It makes your breasts fill out, causes hair to grow under your arms and in your pubic area, and affects your height and weight. At the beginning of each menstrual cycle, the body produces extra estrogen. This signals the womb to get ready for an extra egg. It also increases the flow of LH, which releases the egg from

the two big hormones

the ovary. After ovulation, the body reduces the amount of estrogen being produced.

Progesterone is another important female hormone. It makes the lining of the womb grow so that it can hold a fertilized egg and support the growing baby. If the egg is not fertilized, progesterone levels begin to fall. This is the beginning of the second half of the menstrual cycle Without the extra progesterone, the lining of the womb stops growing, shrivels up, and breaks down. Blood and mucus carry it out of the body during the monthly period.

from childhood to puberty: the outer signs

Going from childhood to puberty is a major event in anyone's life. The changes that take place affect boys as well as girls. Both sexes develop body hair and adult sweat glands, and are more likely to get pimples. Puberty also brings changes that are very different in boys and girls.

Periods are part of the system that allows a woman to have a baby. Although you're too young to think of having a baby, your body is getting ready for future motherhood.

what happens to boys at puberty?

A boy's sexual organs are on the outside of the body. A man's body does not change inside as a result of sexual activity. The shoulders broaden, the voice changes, and hair grows on the face, under the arms, and in the genital area. Oil glands and sweat glands in the skin become active. The testes are able to produce sperm.

What happens to girls at puberty?

The breasts fill out and the hips become wider. Hair begins to grow under the arms and between the legs. The lips of the vagina become fuller and grow closer together. Oil glands and sweat glands in the skin become active. Most of a girl's sexual organs are inside the body. A woman's body can change dramatically when she is pregnant.

periods

from childhood to puberty: the inside story

First, let's get the geography right. Put your thumbs and index fingers together to make an upside-down triangle. Place it against your body between the bottom of your stomach and the top of your legs. That's the space taken up by the sexual organs that together are called the reproductive system. They were all there when you were a baby and they grow bigger as you get older. Here are the details:

You have two ovaries, one at each side of your pelvis, just inside your hips. They look like open baskets about the size and shape of unshelled walnuts. Thousands of tiny eggs are stored here. Leading from the ovaries are two fallopian tubes. Each of these tubes is about four inches (10cm) long and as thick as a piece of spaghetti. When an egg is ripe, it bursts out of the ovary and moves through the fallopian tube and down into the womb.

The pear-shaped womb lies between the two ovaries. It is about three inches (8cm) long. When a woman becomes pregnant, it stretches to hold the baby as it develops. At the bottom of the womb is the cervix. This opens into the vagina. Made of skin, muscle, and fiber-like tissue, the vagina is four to five inches (10–13 cm) long and lies between the lips, or labia, on the outside of the body, and the cervix. When a baby is born, the vagina stretches to allow it to pass from the womb. Then it shrinks back to its original size.

from childhood to puberty:
more on the inside story

Taking a closer look at your sexual organs will give you a better understanding of how they work. Just because your vagina is inside your body doesn't mean you can't look at it. You can do this by sitting on your bed and propping a mirror between your legs so that you can see everything clearly. This may seems strange, but it's perfectly natural to look at your own body.

top-to-toe tip

It's perfectly safe to feel inside your vagina. This is where you will insert tampons if you decide to use them during your period.

First you'll see two flaps of skin, which probably have hair growing on them. These are the outer labia. They are close together to protect the silkier, more delicate skin underneath.

Inside the outer labia are the inner labia. They grow during puberty, becoming slightly darker and more wrinkly. At the top of the point where the inner labia

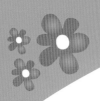

join lies the clitoris. This small mound of skin is very sensitive to touch. When rubbed, it creates pleasurable sexual feelings in a woman, in much the same way as the penis in a man.

Separate the inner labia, and you'll see an opening toward the bottom. This is the vagina. When you insert your finger, you'll feel the moist, stretchy tissue inside.

There is another opening above the vagina. This is the urethra, through which you urinate. Farther down, at the base of your spine and in between the two cheeks of your bottom, is your anus. This is where bowel movements come out of your body.

everything
a girl **needs to know**
about her
periods

periods are good for you

You won't know how you'll feel about your periods until you begin having them. Chances are that you'll feel great! Scientists conducting a study in Boston reported that all women they interviewed said they felt joyful and excited about their body's new powers when they began having periods. Many cultures throughout history have had a different view. Some people used to believe that menstrual blood was poisonous and that women

here are two reasons why

one The monthly period doesn't just get rid of the lining of the womb and the unfertilized egg. It also removes harmful bacteria and helps your immune system.

two Your body is using its resources and energy in the best possible way when it goes through the menstruation process on a regular basis. Sure, it may be a nuisance sometimes. But for most women, periods cause very little trouble. For most of your life, you can be as active and energetic during your period as at any other time.

had to be isolated while they were having periods. Even today, some people behave as though having periods were an illness or embarrassing. It isn't. It's a normal, healthy part of being a woman.

everything
a girl needs to know
about her
periods

your first period

It's one of those unforgettable days. If you are like most women, you will remember for the rest of your life where you were and what you felt like when your first period started. So make the day a good one! Chances are you feel a bit excited anyway, so why not celebrate? You can have a "period party" with just your mother or with a whole gang of friends.

You may have mixed feelings about starting your period. It may come sooner than you would have liked. The idea of having to use sanitary pads or tampons every month may seem a bit overwhelming. And then there's the fact that you're on your way to becoming a woman while still feeling pretty much like a kid!

The best way to deal with all of these changes is to learn how to take care of yourself. What makes you feel better (or worse) during each phase of your cycle? Talking about your period with friends is also helpful, but keep in mind that every girl's experience is different, and you are the only one who knows how your period makes you feel.

the whole month

day-by-day

You may have picked up this book on the very first day of your first period. Or maybe you think you're going to start soon and want to plan ahead. Or you may already have started, and decided that now's the time to get the lowdown on what's happening. Whatever the case, you're in the right place.

This section will describe what happens, how you'll feel, and what you can do for each day of your menstrual cycle. At the end of the section, there is a journal where you can keep track of your period. You can write down how you're feeling emotionally and physically. This will help you know what to expect from your periods in the future.

how much blood will I lose?

Although your blood loss often seems to be heavy, the average is about three to five tablespoonfuls per period.

1

days 1&2 what's happening?

The egg in your uterus (also known as the womb) has just learned there is no sperm waiting to fertilize it. So out it goes, through the cervix and out the vagina, along with blood, mucus, and tissue. This is your period.

You're most likely to have your heaviest blood flow during this time. But it won't always be the same. One month you might have a light flow in the first few days. The next month it may be heavier at the beginning of your period. Don't worry about whether it's heavy or light, or that it changes from month to month. The amount of flow depends on how your body is working at this particular time.

The color and texture of your menstrual flow will vary too. It can be bright red or quite dark. Sometimes it's smooth and liquid, and at other times it might have clumps and clots.

Sometimes it might feel like the flow is very fast, but it isn't. The lining of the womb doesn't come out all at once. It actually breaks down and drips out of the body quite slowly.

days 1&2

what it feels like

Lots of girls feel perfectly fine at this time, apart from a slight stomach ache. But you may find that you don't feel quite as good as usual. The pain that you get in your stomach is caused by hormones called prostaglandins. They make the muscles of the womb contract so that they squeeze out the lining that is no longer needed. Some girls and women seem to have more of these hormones than others. That makes their muscles squeeze faster and harder, and it is probably why they get more pain or cramps.

which pain relievers?

Talk to your doctor, the pharmacist, or ask your mom for advice. There are special medicines designed to ease pain caused by your period.

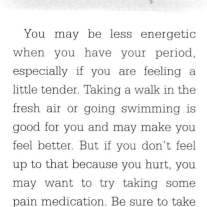

You may be less energetic when you have your period, especially if you are feeling a little tender. Taking a walk in the fresh air or going swimming is good for you and may make you feel better. But if you don't feel up to that because you hurt, you may want to try taking some pain medication. Be sure to take only the dose recommended for pain caused by periods. Then lie down with a hot pad or hot-water bottle on your stomach, and take it easy for a while.

what to do days 1&2

Some girls worry that they smell bad when they have their period. Well, people don't worry that bleeding from a cut on their finger or a bump on their knee is smelly. But still, girls may think the odor is so strong that other people notice it. Some ads even say that girls need to take extra care to "stay fresh" around this time. Well, it's simply not true.

Personal hygiene is important at this time, but as long as you change your pads or tampons regularly, wear clean panties, and keep your body clean, you won't smell any different than you usually do. If blood soaks through onto your panties, change them as soon as possible. Wash them in cold water and salt to prevent stains. Wash yourself, too.

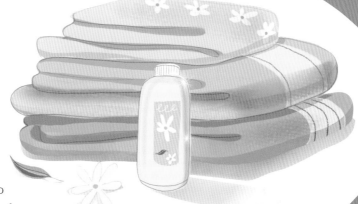

Never use perfumed sprays around the genital area. They can irritate your skin. It's a good idea to have a shower or bath every day when you're having a period, because you may sweat a little more than usual. If you are feeling tender or stressed out, take a long soak in the bathtub—it's better than a shower (find out why in the help! section of this book).

top-to-toe tip

Don't worry that a bath will stop your period. It won't affect the flow or hurt you at all.

everything
a girl needs to know
about her
periods

days 3&4
what's happening?

These are the days when your body is forcing out the rest of the lining and tissue from your womb.

Periods usually last between five and seven days, but it is normal for them to vary a lot, especially in teenage girls. You may still have quite a heavy flow, or it may have finished. Your next period may be longer, shorter, or exactly the same length as this one.

days 3&4

what it feels like
exercising during your period

Any kind of active sport, like swimming, running, aerobics, or tennis, helps your circulation and prevents cramps. Even walking briskly for half an hour will do the trick—so forget the school bus or your usual ride, and walk, even though it's the last thing you feel like doing. Exercise that relaxes you (and your muscles) will also help. Yoga is very popular with girls and

women. It reduces tension and stress, helping your mind as well as your body.

"I'm having my period." Girls have used that excuse for getting out of gym for years. If it doesn't work, be grateful. Girls who exercise regularly get less period pain.

Here's what to do

one Stand very straight. Imagine that someone is pulling up on a thread that runs up from your heels, through your spine, and out through the top of your head.

two Pull in your tummy muscles and breathe deeply.

three Keep this posture for as long as you can—all day if possible.

stretching—low impact exercise

Exercising when you have a period can make you bleed slightly more than usual. Be sure to change your pad or tampon before you start your exercise.

what to do days 3&4

If you're still bleeding—and most girls will be—remember that you'll need tampons or pads every day. It's a good idea to keep some in your school locker or in your purse. That way you'll be prepared if you forget to grab them when you rush out of the house in the morning.

When you have a heavy flow, it can seem like you are losing pints of blood. In fact, it's quite rare for anyone to lose more than a few tablespoonfuls. However, if your pads or tampons become drenched every hour, discuss it with your mom, the school nurse, or a health-care worker.

If you run out of tampons or pads and don't have any money to buy more, don't be afraid of asking for help from a friend or the school office. A tightly wrapped wad of toilet paper can always be used in an emergency!

top-to-toe tip

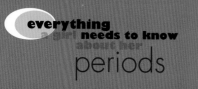

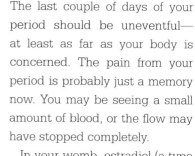

The last couple of days of your period should be uneventful—at least as far as your body is concerned. The pain from your period is probably just a memory now. You may be seeing a small amount of blood, or the flow may have stopped completely.

In your womb, estradiol (a type of estrogen) is released and causes the lining of the womb to thicken as it prepares to receive a fertilized egg. This process of creating a "nest" for the egg continues over many days of your cycle (it takes about 12 days).

days 5 to 7

what's happening?

everything
a girl needs to know
about her
periods

days 5 to 7

what it feels like

It's quite normal to be bleeding for a whole week. By day seven, the flow should at least be slowing down, and stop within the next day or so. If you have heavy periods for a week or longer, especially if you also have bad menstrual pain the whole time, you should talk to a health-care worker.

Keep that journal up to date! You may think that you'll remember the pattern of your period, but the chances are you won't—trust us! Filling in the chart takes a couple of minutes and it's really worth it.

top-to-toe tip

days 5 to 7

what to do
toxic shock syndrome

If you are using tampons and the flow has almost stopped, you probably should switch to pads or panty liners. Your vagina may be drier than earlier in the period, and it can be irritated if you use a tampon that is too absorbent. It also raises the very slight risk of getting something called toxic shock syndrome (TSS).

Toxic shock syndrome is a group of symptoms caused by bacteria that can grow in the vagina. It can occur in women who wear tampons. Understanding the causes of TSS can help protect you from getting it.

TSS is very rare, but it is slightly more common in teenagers than in older women. If it does occur, it can be serious. Antibiotics will get rid of the bacteria that causes TSS, but you may need to go to the Emergency Room for treatment. The symptoms include a high fever, aching muscles, vomiting, and diarrhea.

TSS happens when the tampon is too absorbent for the amount of blood. This is why it's important not to use tampons that are "super absorbent" when you are not bleeding heavily. Instead, use a tampon with the lowest possible absorbency or switch to pads. Also, change your tampon at least every four hours.

Here's how to check whether the tampon you use has the right absorbency. If, after four hours' use, the tampon has white areas or is still dry, it's probably more absorbent than you need.

7 8 9

6

2

days 8&9

what's happening?

Phew, what a relief! Your period's over. No more blood; no more cramps. If you've had zits, they'll probably disappear now. If you've had an upset stomach during your period, it will clear up too. You'll also find that your panties are the cleanest ever. The mucus that is discharged by the vagina during most of your menstrual cycle stops entirely for a few days.

Of course, your cycle is still active. At around the time your period finishes, your body starts to produce more estrogen and the ovaries start to prepare another egg for release into the fallopian tube. The eggs are in tiny pods called follicles. About 20 follicles begin to ripen the eggs inside them. Your body doesn't yet know whether the chosen egg will come from the left or right ovary. Usually, the ovaries alternate each month.

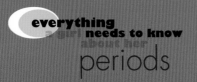

everything needs to know
a girl about her
periods

days 8&9 what it feels like

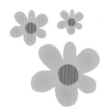

With estrogen levels rising, you're likely to feel full of energy now. And it's good to know that you won't have to bother about tampons or pads during the next week or two. Have fun and enjoy this time between periods.

days 8&9

what to do

Because you know you'll be feeling good, this is a great time to get out and get going, working and playing hard. This is particularly good advice if you find that life gets a little more difficult in the second half of your cycle.

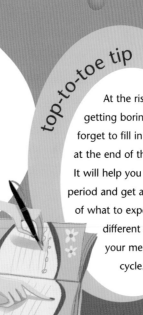

top-to-toe tip

At the risk of
getting boring, don't
forget to fill in the chart
at the end of this section.
It will help you track your
period and get a better idea
of what to expect during
different stages of
your menstrual
cycle.

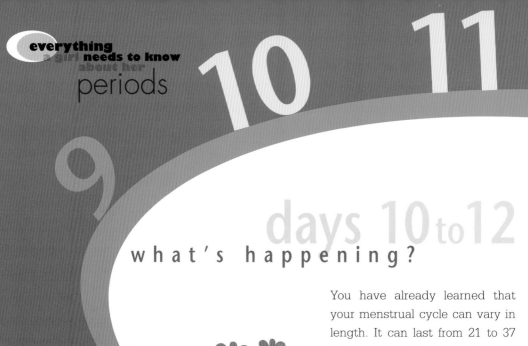

10   11
9

days 10 to 12

what's happening?

You have already learned that your menstrual cycle can vary in length. It can last from 21 to 37 days, or sometimes even longer. For some girls, the cycle is almost always longer or shorter than the average of 28 days. For others, the length of their cycle changes every month.

Usually, this variation occurs in the first half of the cycle (which is

why periods aren't always predictable

approximately the time that this day-by-day account has covered so far). In other words, by days 10 to 12, you might be close to getting your period. Or you might still be weeks away.

It's very common for teenage girls to have long and irregular cycles. Periods become more regular after your body has completed all the changes puberty brings.

There are a number of things that can cause your cycle to last longer than usual. For instance, your body may take longer to release an egg when you have a bad case of flu. The menstrual cycle is much more predictable after an egg has been released. Once that happens, it usually takes two weeks to complete the rest of the cycle.

days 10 to 12

what it feels like

You're feeling your normal, energetic self, while deep down inside of you things are continuing to happen. The contest to choose the one egg that will travel to your uterus is almost over. By about day 12, the "winner" is chosen. One follicle begins to grow while the others, and the eggs inside them, begin to wither.

Of course, you don't feel any of this going on, but there is a way you can track the changing levels of hormones in your body as it prepares for ovulation. The discharge that you find in your panties is a good indicator of your hormone levels. As your progesterone increases, the discharge will change from a sticky

substance to one that has a creamier texture. Then, once hormone levels have peaked and begun to decline (by day 12), it will change again. It will become watery and white, and there will be more of it.

Expect to feel especially good at this time. Of course you are more than your hormones and you can feel great every day of the month. Right now, however, the surge in hormones boosts the feel-good factor for both mind and body.

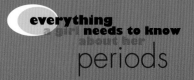

everything a girl needs to know about her periods

days 10 to 12

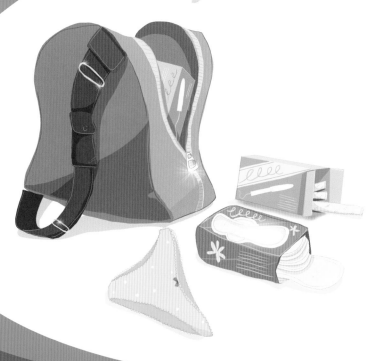

what to do

Many girls find that a "period pack" is a useful and handy thing to have around. Stock the pack with extra pads or tampons, medicine that helps with pain, an extra pair of underwear, comfort food snacks that you like, and any other items that you find to be useful. Keep the pack in your backpack or in your locker at school.

The best time to restock your period pack is when your period is ending. That way, it will be all ready for the next time you need it.

Don't forget to keep that journal up to date. You may think you'll remember how you felt a month ago, but you'd be surprised how difficult it is to pinpoint the exact day you had cramps or some other symptom.

days 13&14

what's happening?

For girls who have a regular cycle, ovulation occurs at some time during these two days—approximately the mid-point of the menstrual cycle. However, it doesn't always happen at this time. In fact, sometimes it doesn't always happen at all. It's quite common not to ovulate during a single cycle.

If you feel extra-aware of the outside world, you're not imagining it. Your vision and sense of smell are sharpest at this time in your cycle.

When you do ovulate, the ovary releases the mature egg (or sometimes two) into the fallopian tube. After ovulation, if the egg isn't fertilized by a sperm, the amount of estrogen in your body falls.

The release of the egg is the high point of activity in the menstrual cycle. But don't expect fireworks! Most girls and women haven't a clue that anything out of the ordinary is happening.

everything **needs to know**
a girl about her
periods

days 13&14

what it feels like

Here are a few signs of ovulation you may notice.

• A dull pain or cramp in the pit of your stomach. For some girls, the cramps are more painful than for others.

• A small amount of bleeding may occur (usually at the same time as the pain).

• Discharge from your vagina increases and becomes thinner and clearer like a raw egg white.

Some scientists believe that women release small amounts of hormones into the air as ovulation time approaches. These airborne hormones are called pheromones. Although they can't be seen or smelled, it is thought that they act as invisible signals that let men know that a woman is fertile, and cause her to appear more attractive.

This theory has never been proved right or wrong, but you may feel very friendly, and want to flirt at this time of

Some research suggests that a woman's closest friends and female relatives are also sensitive to her pheromones, so much so, in fact, that their ovulation might be influenced by these signals. If this theory is true, it could explain why many girls have their periods at the same time as their moms, sisters, or best friends.

the month. Even girls who are far too young to have a baby may feel more bubbly now. It's great to know there is a time when you can depend on those feel-good sensations.

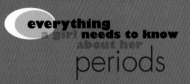

what to do days 13 & 14

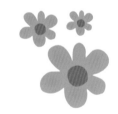

A small percentage of women and girls may experience cramps during this time. More will experience the cramps later on in the cycle (see pages 94–95). Luckily for all, they rarely last longer than six to eight hours. If you do feel crampy, here are some suggestions for relief.

• Rest. Going to bed early or an afternoon nap can make all the difference in how you feel.

• Drink at least eight glasses of water a day.

• Take a long, hot bath—the warmth helps to relieve the pain. Afterward, lie down and read a book, watch TV, or listen to music.

• Use a heating pad or hot water bottle; the heat relaxes the muscles and will bring relief.

• Take a pain reliever, like ibuprofen, that is particularly good for menstrual cramps.

This is also a time to enjoy life. With your senses on high alert, you may want to do things that take advantage of your heightened abilities. Cook up a special meal. Take a walk in the park. Go hiking with friends. The tastes, sounds, smells, and sights will be extra pleasurable.

days 15 & 16

what's happening?

top-to-toe tip

All this activity
raises your body
temperature by about one
degree. This is a tiny increase
but you might feel warmer
than usual in bed at night.
During the day you might
feel more comfortable in
lighter clothing.

It's the beginning of the second half of your menstrual cycle, and the activity in the reproductive organs may slightly change the way you feel. A single mature egg has made its way down the fallopian tube. If the egg was not fertilized by a sperm, the endometrium, or inner lining of the uterus, breaks down and will be shed later in your cycle as a menstrual flow or, as you've come to know it, your period.

In the ovary, the follicle that released the egg is empty. It now becomes known as the *corpus luteum*, Latin for "yellow body," which it soon resembles as it makes greater amounts of hormones, mainly progesterone.

Like all hormones, progesterone flows through the bloodstream to all parts of the body. It makes the lining of the womb soft and

thick—just the cozy surroundings that will be needed later on in your life to protect and feed an embryo. The rising levels of hormones also affect the rest of your body. These hormones help to keep your bones strong and your heart, kidneys, pancreas, and brain healthy, too.

days 15 & 16

what it feels like

When your period starts, you might notice some changes throughout your body, especially in your breasts. The whoosh of hormones around your body at this stage of the menstrual cycle sometimes causes the breasts to swell a little. They might also become tender. It's usually a mild sensation. You may feel more aware of your breasts than usual or they might feel a bit heavy. Sometimes the breasts become really uncomfortable or even painful. Don't worry about it—

there's actually nothing wrong. And there are things you can do to help ease the pain (see pages 72–73).

Lots of girls have complicated feelings about their breasts. Most people feel self-conscious about body parts that attract a lot of attention from others. This is specially true when you are just getting used to the way your body is changing. Girls worry that their breasts are too big or too small. Well, there isn't just one size that is right for everyone. Your breasts are just right for you.

Talking about your feelings with a trusted adult or laughing with friends about some of the silly reactions you've had from other people is a healthy way to deal with these concerns.

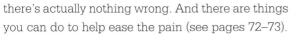

top-to-toe tip

everything **needs to know**
a girl needs to know about her
periods

days 15 & 16

w h a t   t o   d o

dealing with breast pain

Most teenage girls won't have breast pain during their period. It's more likely to happen to women in their late twenties or thirties, and many women never have the problem at all. However, if you do get breast pain, here are five ways to deal with it:

one Buy a bra that fits well and holds your breasts firmly, especially if you have large breasts. Good support won't cure the pain, but it will let you move about as energetically as you wish to, without making the discomfort worse.

two Avoid drinks that have a lot of caffeine, like coffee, tea, and cola. Lots of girls find that breast pain disappears when they stop drinking caffeine.

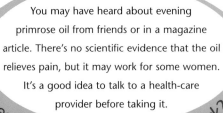

You may have heard about evening primrose oil from friends or in a magazine article. There's no scientific evidence that the oil relieves pain, but it may work for some women. It's a good idea to talk to a health-care provider before taking it.

does evening primrose oil work?

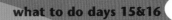

three Drink lots of water. If your body is storing too much water, breast pain can be the result. The best way to get rid of excess water is to drink more liquid. This stimulates the kidneys to eliminate the extra fluid.

four Stay active. Good blood circulation will prevent your breasts from becoming swollen and tender.

five If the pain is really bad, take an anti-inflammatory medicine, such as ibuprofen.

days 17 to 20
what's happening?

At this point in your cycle, your body is preparing to receive a fertilized egg. Also known as post-ovulation, it is the time that progesterone is on the increase and estrogen levels are dropping. With these changes taking place, let's remember what these hormones are and what they do.

Estrogen is at the highest level in your body just before an ovary releases an egg. After that, it begins to fall. This hormone plays a major role in keeping the bones strong and the heart healthy. However, it can also cause bloating in the stomach and breast pain (see pages 92–93 and 72–73).

Progesterone levels increase after the ovary releases the egg. This hormone prepares the womb for a baby and acts as a natural antidepressant. Changes in levels of this hormone can cause mood swings before your period starts.

Prostaglandin is released about 10 days before your period starts. This hormone causes the womb to contract, forcing the unfertilized egg and other material into the vagina. Too much of the hormone, however, can also cause cramps in your back or stomach at this time of the month.

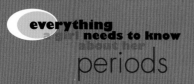

everything a girl needs to know about her
periods

w h a t   i t   f e e l s   l i k e

The effects of the rise and fall of the progesterone and estrogen hormones may show themselves now as an increased feeling of bloating or water retention, breast tenderness, moodiness, and cramping.

top-to-toe tip

Keeping a record of your
feelings during this time is so
important! This can be a topsy-turvy time,
so use the chart at the back of this section to
record your moods, emotional reactions, and
physical symptoms. Did you feel lonely,
embarrassed, angry, hurt? What worked, what
didn't? Write it down! If you note your feelings
and reactions, you can chart how your
period affects your moods and maybe
avoid uncomfortable situations
the next time around.

days 17 to 2

what to do

The change in hormones during the menstrual cycle affects some girls quite dramatically and others not at all. If you are in the first group, the symptoms may appear about 10 days before your next period is due to start.

Sometimes, the best treatment for these symptoms is to find someone with a sympathetic ear—your mom, best friend, maybe an older sister—someone you can talk with and share experiences. But simple dietary changes, exercise, and relaxation can also work wonders for you. In terms of diet, here are some suggestions:

• Try to have less fat, sugar, salt, and caffeine.

• Try to have more starch, fiber, vegetables, and fruit (see the food chart on pages 136–137).

top-to-toe tip

Some women feel so bad at this time of the month that it interferes with their normal life. This is called premenstrual syndrome (PMS). It doesn't happen as often as people think and girls your age don't usually have it.

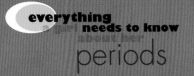

18 19 20

days 21 & 22

what's happening?

This is the time in the month when progesterone rises to its highest level in your bloodstream. The progesterone allows the uterus to build up supplies of protein, sugar, and blood—ingredients necessary to nourish a fertilized egg.

Remember LH and FSH (page 16)? These are the hormones that start the menstrual cycle. After ovulation, the amount of LH and FSH in your bloodstream starts to drop. Estrogen is at a low point. If a sperm doesn't fertilize the egg in the fallopian tube, the production of progesterone will fall, too.

21 22

Without progesterone, the lining of the womb stops growing. It begins to shrivel and break down. Soon the body will shed the lining and the rest of the unwanted material in the womb. From now until your period starts, these hormones fall to their lowest point.

are there any signs of what's happening?

Once again, the best indicator that you've reached this stage of the menstrual cycle is the discharge on the crotch of your panties. Suddenly, there will be less of it, and it will become thicker and creamier in texture.

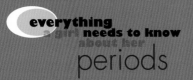

days 21 & 22

what it feels like

Some girls experience extreme emotions during this time of the month. They can be prone to door slamming, foot-stomping, and sudden tearful outbursts.

But it is also true that some, if not most, girls and women feel fine at this time. In fact, some feel better than ever—we just don't hear much about them.

top-to-toe-tip

Feel like having a good cry? Go ahead. Tears can be cleansing.

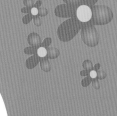

Don't assume that the way your sister or your girlfriends feel at this point in the cycle will be the same for you. Everyone is different.

top-to-toe tip

what to do days 21 & 22

Compared to the first half of the menstrual cycle (during which girls often feel bubbly, outgoing, and full of fun), the second half can seem quite different.

Instead of focusing your energy on everyone else, you may find that you're more thoughtful and inward-looking. In turn, this can make you feel more vulnerable, even sad. You may be less willing to join in noisy or lively group activities. Saying "no thanks" firmly but politely is often the best way to deal with invitations when you're feeling like this.

your moods

Other demands on your time or your emotional energy can also be unwelcome. You may feel that all you want is to be left alone in your own private space.

Learning to go with the flow is probably the most important lesson for dealing with these changing emotions. Be aware of what your feelings are. Let yourself be guided by them rather than getting upset or being annoyed. Ease your way through this sensitive time, and give yourself plenty of space when you're feeling easily upset.

your energy levels

Just as your emotions may change at this time of the month, so might your energy levels. If you are active in sports, you might suddenly find that a workout or activity that seemed easy a week or so ago has suddenly become a lot more difficult.

Scientists have learned that when estrogen levels fall in the second half of the cycle, the muscles get their fuel from food more slowly. Because of this, they don't work as fast or as easily at this time. You may sometimes feel like you have a totally different body, one that's tired and sluggish.

On the other hand, you may find that your energy levels stay the same throughout the whole of your cycle. This is true for lots of girls.

top-to-toe tip

Feeling tired now doesn't mean you should stop exercising or go to bed for a week every month. Let "slow down but keep going" be your motto.

everything
a girl needs to know
about her
periods

days 23&24 what's happening?

severe symptoms

People talk about premenstrual syndrome (PMS) as if most girls and women get it. In fact, PMS is quite rare—it affects only two or three in every 100 women, and it almost never affects teenagers.

It's important to recognize the difference between having PMS and experiencing a few of the premenstrual symptoms that you'll read about in this book. That's why we'll look at PMS closely, even though it's unlikely that you'll have it.

People get confused because a lot of premenstrual symptoms (page 13) are also symptoms of PMS. The difference is that while most girls and women may complain about such symptoms, they can still go about their normal lives. Girls and women who have PMS find that it seriously disrupts their ability to function. PMS not only robs them of energy, but it also prevents them from doing the everyday things they usually do quite easily.

who gets PMS?

If you think most of your friends get PMS, think again. The chances are that not a single girl in your class has this problem.

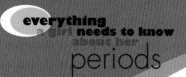

what it feels like days 23 & 24

about PMS

PMS has hundreds of possible symptoms. You may have some of them from time to time. But women with PMS have at least five of the following symptoms the week before their periods, and they are so severe that they interfere with normal daily activities.

emotional symptoms

• Mood swings: You feel happy, then sad, then angry in the same day (or even the same hour), without really knowing why.

• Irritability: You snap at friends for things that usually wouldn't bother you.

• Anxiety: You worry about things that aren't really that important.

• Depression: You feel sad a lot of the time or cry over the smallest thing.

• Listlessness: You lose interest in things. None of the hobbies or sports you usually like sound fun any more. You may not even like your friends.

physical symptoms

• Fatigue: You often feel like falling asleep, even in the middle of the day.

• Disturbed sleep: You sleep too much or wake up a lot in the middle of the night.

• Breast pain: Your breasts feel puffy and sore.

• Bloating: Your waist measurement increases and you feel uncomfortable. Your ankles and fingers may swell, too.

• Headaches: They're severe and they last a long time.

In addition, you may have problems concentrating or find yourself craving certain foods.

days 23&24

what to do

Here are some symptoms that are quite common in the week before a period. But don't worry—you're very unlikely to have all of them, and there are always ways to make yourself feel better.

headaches

You may never have had a headache until your first period. Headaches, particularly very severe ones called migraines, can be caused by the drop in estrogen and progesterone, just before a period.

what to do

• Cut back on salt. Salt helps the body store extra water. This can cause headaches, so cut out or reduce the amount of salt you eat. Cut back or avoid salty snacks like potato chips, nuts, and pretzels.

• Consider taking a pain reliever. If the headaches occur with almost every cycle, talk to your health-care provider about taking aspirin or ibuprofen daily in the week before your period.

the good news on headaches

If you didn't have a headache just before or during your first period, then you probably won't ever get a menstrual headache. Headaches that come and go with the menstrual cycle nearly always start with the first period.

top-to-toe tip

Record-keeping is really helpful at this stage of your cycle. Recognizing patterns of premenstrual symptoms means you can take action to stop them from happening.

50mg

days 23&24

more what to do

sleeplessness

It's common for girls to have their sleep disrupted during their periods. Often other symptoms, such as headaches or cramps, keep them awake.

what to do

• Treat other symptoms so that they don't interfere with your sleep patterns.

• Get into the habit of going to bed and getting up at the same time during this week.

• Get plenty of exercise and fresh air, even if you're feeling sluggish, and don't take naps.

zits

For some girls and women, the arrival of pimples or acne that gets worse is a sign that a period is on its way. The oil ducts under the skin that cause acne are fully open between days 21 and 26 of a 28-day menstrual cycle.

what to do

There's no special treatment for zits that appear around this time. Just keep washing your face with a mild cleanser.

bloating

If you have bloating, you're not alone. This symptom affects one out of two women in the week before a period. Your tummy becomes slightly swollen and tender, and you feel uncomfortable and have gas. Bloating has several causes. Hormones share some of the blame. Eating too much of the wrong kind of food can also lead to bloating.

what to do

• Keep a food diary. Use it to help you identify foods that may cause this unpleasant symptom. Look at ways to improve your diet and check out the food chart on pages 136–137.

• Drink lots of water. The more you drink, the more fluid will be flushed out of your system.

• Keep moving. Exercise helps your digestion and also flushes excess water out of your system.

days 23&24

more what to do

cramps

Most women get cramps before or during their periods. Often, the cramps only cause mild discomfort. Some teenage girls do get really strong cramps, however, and the pain spreads from the stomach around to the lower back.

Cramps are caused in part by hormones. No one likes getting them, but almost all women do. At least you know you have lots of company, and that cramps are a normal part of the menstrual cycle.

what to do

See pages 66 and 67 for relief suggestions.

top-to-toe tip

Exercising regularly all through the month
is one of the best ways to reduce cramps.

teeth alert

The inside of your mouth and your gums can become more sensitive as you reach puberty. After you begin menstruating, your gums may swell, become tender, and bleed more easily in the week before your period.

what to do

Really good dental hygiene will help to keep this symptom under control. As well as brushing and flossing your teeth every day, you should see a dentist regularly.

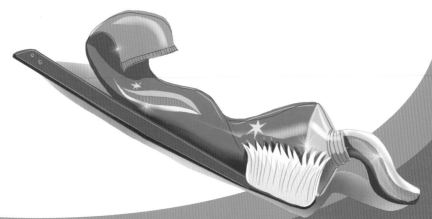

days 25&26
what's happening?

The amount of hormones being produced in your body has been falling. Progesterone and estrogen have almost reached their lowest levels at this point. This usually means that there will also be low levels of the hormones that make us feel good, serotonin and beta-endorphins.

When and how fast progesterone and estrogen levels fall may have something to do with your premenstrual symptoms. If progesterone drops very quickly, at, say, day 21, and then stays very low until your period starts, then it's likely that you'll get more (or stronger) symptoms. The opposite seems to be true of estrogen. If estrogen levels are high all the way up to the day your period starts, then a sudden drop in estrogen levels will, more than likely, make you feel worse.

The bad news is you can't do anything about it. Knowing what's happening, though, means that at least you can blame your hormones if you're feeling rotten, and sometimes that helps.

so what can I do about it?

days 25&26

what it feels like

You might not be able to avoid premenstrual symptoms, but there are things you can do to feel better. Regular exercise and getting plenty of sleep are two of them. Here are some more.

making yourself feel better

one Be aware of your stress levels and try to pace your life in a way that reduces stress as much as possible. You can't organize your life so that tests or break-ups with friends never happen in the week before your period. But keep in mind that you, like other girls, are more likely to be sensitive to stress around this time. The next two tips can help keep stress under control.

two Relax your body. Sometimes simply vegging out in front of the TV can do the trick. Or treat yourself to time on the sofa with a favorite magazine or book. Make yourself comfortable and take time to enjoy some music.

three Try a yoga or t'ai chi class. All that delicious stretching and mind–body focus can leave you feeling much clearer and looser.

four Pamper yourself. This is especially important when you feel underappreciated by other people. Do your nails or perhaps braid your hair.

days 25&26
what to do

vitamins or minerals?

Some people believe that premenstrual problems are a result of not having enough vitamins or minerals. They say that taking extra vitamins and minerals throughout the month, or for the last two weeks of the menstrual cycle, can make a big difference. Some pills combine vitamins and minerals that are thought to work especially well in treating premenstrual symptoms. Other pills contain just one vitamin or mineral. Opposite are the three main ones.

calcium

Calcium is thought to bring relief from mood swings, food cravings, bloating, headaches, and cramps. Taking extra calcium has been shown to relieve symptoms for about half the women who've tried it. Calcium is also found in dairy products, canned fish, dried fruit, and nuts.

vitamin B6

This vitamin appears to improve premenstrual symptoms, particularly bad moods. It reduces the amount of estrogen and increases the level of progesterone in the blood. B6 is found in raw fruit, fish, meat, and chicken.

magnesium

Magnesium is thought to reduce mood swings. It seems to work by activating serotonin, a substance that helps to stabilize our emotions. It does not seem to have as strong an effect as calcium or vitamin B6. Green vegetables, fruit, whole-wheat foods, nuts, seeds, and peanut butter contain magnesium.

everything
a girl needs to know
about her
periods

getting help

If you go to a health-care provider,
take along your menstrual journal. The journal will
enable you to describe your symptoms more accurately.
It will make it a lot easier for the doctor or
nurse to help you.

days 25&26
more what to do

using pain relievers

You don't have to suffer from pain. Some over-the-counter medicines, like ibuprofen and aspirin, can relieve headaches, backaches, and cramps. Others are aimed at a number of other problems that may bother you during your period. These kinds of pain relievers are safe and effective for most people. Ask your mother, or a nurse, doctor, or pharmacist for advice about which ones are best for you.

Don't take diuretics—pills that make you urinate more—to relieve bloating. They can cause your body to lose too much fluid (become dehydrated) and essential minerals. This will only make your symptoms worse.

Some girls find that nothing seems to work. They regularly get monster cramps and other symptoms. If that's you, it's definitely worthwhile seeing a school nurse or other health-care worker. You may have an underlying health problem, or you may just need a stronger pain reliever, which a doctor can prescribe.

days 27 & 28

what's happening?

The menstrual cycle is ending. Levels of estrogen and progesterone in the womb have fallen to almost nothing, causing two important things to occur.

First, the lining of the womb has broken down and is ready to be shed.

Second, the brain produces GnRH, which leads to the release of FSH and LH (page 16). This means the whole cycle is ready to start again.

top-to-toe tip

Notice what's happening to your emotions. If one day you feel tired, cross, and unlovable, and the next day your period starts, try to laugh about it (and write it down in the journal pages!). The right attitude could make next month a whole lot easier.

How you feel during these two days can vary. If you are like most girls, you will have some stomach cramps, which can be a useful tip-off that your period is about to begin. Some girls do experience more severe cramping and get headaches as well. Still others (lucky them!) experience almost no discomfort at all.

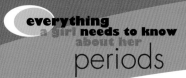

days 27&28
what it feels like

tummy trouble

It's not unusual for girls to have diarrhea around this time. Pain associated with your period can make the body produce substances that relax the smooth muscle of the intestine. This makes it difficult for your intestine to hold onto food for the proper amount of time. The hormonal changes now occurring can also cause diarrhea.

what you can do

Treat your tummy gently. Instead of rough, tough foods, choose natural binders such as white rice, pasta, potatoes, and bananas. Eat small meals several times a day.

Here we go again: drink lots of water! Health experts recommend that you drink about eight eight-ounce (250ml) glasses of water a day, which is especially important if you're not feeling well. It may seem a lot, but if you start with a glass of water first thing in the morning, and try to remember to drink another glass every hour or so during the rest of the day, the benefits will add up.

top-to-toe tip

If you have very bad diarrhea, check
with your doctor. You may need to take rehydration
fluid, available from the pharmacy.

days 27&28 what to do

getting physical

This is probably not the time of the month to start training for a marathon. But even on days when you're most likely to have premenstrual symptoms, you'll feel better if you get moving. Low-impact aerobic activities, such as walking, cycling, yoga, or gentle stretching, reduce stress in your breasts and your stomach. You'll feel better physically.

There are other benefits, too. With regular

exercise, you'll feel more alert and more in control. You'll be less likely to have mood swings, and you'll sleep better. You might even have fewer cravings for sugary, fatty foods.

Just 10 minutes of gentle exercise will make a difference in how you feel. Thirty minutes or longer will be even more satisfying.

Put on soothing music and wear comfortable clothes. Lie on the floor or sit in a comfortable chair and try not to think about anything. Then concentrate on relaxing your muscles. Start with your feet. When they're relaxed, focus on your legs. Work your way up to your face and scalp. Pay special attention to the muscles around your stomach.

top-to-toe tip

more what to do days 27 & 28

talk, talk, talk

By now, you may have found that talking about what you've been through when you've had your period isn't always easy. You may have mixed feelings about the whole experience, and that is normal. Maybe you feel proud of the fact that you have your period or maybe you feel a little embarrassed, but not sure why. It may make you feel funny to think that others know, especially boys. Parents want to be supportive of their daughters when they start their periods, but some are shy about discussing the subject. Sometimes it can even be difficult to talk to girlfriends about an experience that's not just new, but also private and personal.

Do it anyway. There's a huge amount of information and understanding out there that you can get from others, not just from health professionals but from other women—moms, aunts, older sisters, and friends.

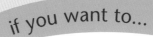

if you want to...

• Know something, then ask. Your mom may be longing to talk to you and is just waiting for the right time.

• Share something, then speak your mind. Being cool has its place, but your friends will appreciate it if you talk honestly about how you feel—and they'll almost certainly want to join in with their own experiences.

• Express something, then let it out! Laughing about difficult things is a great way of coping. And having a good cry can be healing, too.

journal
keeping a record

On the next three pages there is a journal to use for recording one cycle of your menstrual period. You can also use this format in a separate journal and keep it over a time of several months. Start the journal on the first day of your period—"day 1"—and add in the date. In the extra space you can make a note about how you're feeling emotionally and physically.

What will you get out of it? By using the journal, you should start to feel a little more in control. Periods are going to happen almost every month until you're a woman of 50 or so. By keeping a record over a few months or even over a year, a pattern will gradually emerge. You'll learn the signs that tell you that your period is due, and you'll know how your feelings change during the menstrual cycle. If you sometimes feel a little below par, at least you'll know it will quickly pass. And you can look forward to the high points of the cycle, too.

day 1   date   I feel...

day 2   date   I feel...

day 3   date   I feel...

day 4   date   I feel...

day 5   date   I feel...

day 6   date   I feel...

day 7   date   I feel...

day 8   date   I feel...

day 9   date   I feel...

day 10   date   I feel...

periods

day 11   date   I feel...

day 12   date   I feel...

day 13   date   I feel...

day 14   date   I feel...

day 15   date   I feel...

day 16   date   I feel...

day 17   date   I feel...

day 18   date   I feel...

day 19   date   I feel...

day 20   date   I feel...

day 21   date   I feel...

day 22   date   I feel...

day 23   date   I feel...

day 24   date   I feel...

day 25   date   I feel...

day 26   date   I feel...

day 27   date   I feel...

day 28   date   I feel...

notes

help! answers to your questions

Having your period is a whole new experience for you but don't feel shy about asking for advice. Every woman has gone through the same things that are happening to you now. Your mom, aunt, or older sister will probably be happy to share with you how they handled a particular situation.

You can also use this book to do some research on your own. On the following pages you will find answers to some of the most common questions girls ask about their periods. You will learn how to put in a tampon with step-by-step instructions and will also find out about diet, things you can do to feel better, and other topics that you may find helpful.

help!

how many periods will I have?

Here is some really surprising information! As you may know, a woman's period stops when she's pregnant and doesn't start again until a few months after the birth. Let's imagine that when you're an adult, you get pregnant twice and have two children. If this is the case, then you'll have about 420 periods during the course of your life. That means you will menstruate for more than 2,000 days, a total of nearly six years!

And here are more interesting facts. By the time you were born, your ovaries had about 400,000 eggs. During your life, 400 to 500 eggs will ripen and be released into your womb. As we have seen, you will have a period each time an egg ripens and doesn't get fertilized.

It's clear that having periods is going to be a long-term proposition and that they will be a part of your life until you stop menstruating. But that doesn't mean periods have to take over your life. By reading this book, you are taking a giant step toward learning how your cycle works and how to feel good about being a woman.

help!

my periods aren't regular

Don't worry if your periods are irregular at first. Chances are they will become more regular as time goes on. The hormones that control your menstrual cycle don't suddenly start working perfectly. They take time to get established, sometimes as long as three or four years.

The length of your period may also vary. Sometimes a period lasts just two or three days. Other times you will continue to flow for a whole week. Usually, the bleeding is heaviest at the beginning of the period. After a day or two, it becomes lighter. There may be just a little spotting during the last couple of days.

Even when periods are regular, menstrual cycles can vary a lot. The average cycle takes from 28 to 31 days, but some women have 21-day cycles while others have cycles that go on for as long as 36 days.

do I need to see a doctor about irregular periods?

Only if they continue to be irregular over several years or if you find that they are suddenly becoming less frequent. Irregular periods can be a sign that a woman is suffering from stress. They can result from gaining or losing too much weight. Very rarely, they are a sign of more serious illness.

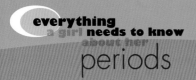

help!

what if I don't have a period?

Don't jump to conclusions. It's very common for girls who start having periods in their early teens to have them very irregularly until they are about 18 years old. However, there are times when you should see a health-care provider about your periods. These include:

You're 16 and your periods haven't started. There's probably no need to check with a doctor until you're 18, but if you're worried, a doctor's opinion might reassure you.

You haven't had a period for several months. Dieting, exercising a lot, or stress at home or at school can affect your menstrual cycle. Discuss missed periods with a school nurse or a doctor to find out what to do.

Your periods are irregular, and you have a very bad case of acne and more body hair than normal. These are signs that you may have tiny cysts (like pimples) in the ovaries. If so, you will need to see a specialist who will know how to treat this condition.

help!

my periods are too heavy

It's quite normal for periods to be heavy and contain clots for up to four or five days. However, if you have heavy periods for longer than this or if cramps prevent you from taking part in your usual activities, see a health-care provider. Sometimes all you need is reassurance that you are okay. If a medical problem is causing the heavy bleeding, the doctor will treat it.

Here are three ways to help reduce the pain and even the blood flow of a heavy period:

one Exercise at least three times a week.

two Eat a balanced diet. Include fresh fruit and vegetables, fish, and sunflower or olive oil.

three Take the appropriate pain-relieving medication.

The main thing is not to suffer in silence. Talk to someone in your family, or perhaps a counselor or school nurse about the way you are feeling. Don't forget to record in your journal when you get each period, how heavy it is, and any symptoms.

help!

what should I wear— a tampon or a pad?

There are so many products that it may be hard for you to choose what to use when you have a period. The main choice is between sanitary pads, which are also called napkins, and tampons.

Both pads and tampons are comfortable and easy to use—and nobody can tell you're wearing them. Read the information on the next pages to help you decide which suits you best.

Pads stick to the inside of your panties. They soak up the blood as it leaves your body. They're usually made of soft cotton and have a plastic covering on the bottom.

Tampons fit inside your vagina and absorb the blood before it leaves your body. They're made of cotton, too. Some come in plastic or cardboard tubes that make it easier for you to put the tampon inside your vagina. You can insert other types by using your

how many a day?

Whether you use pads or tampons, you need to change them several times a day. You can tell when a pad needs changing simply by looking at it. Change a tampon at least every four hours.

finger. All tampons have a string at one end so that they're easy to pull out when they need changing.

Most pads and tampons are made to be used only once. Others can be reused.

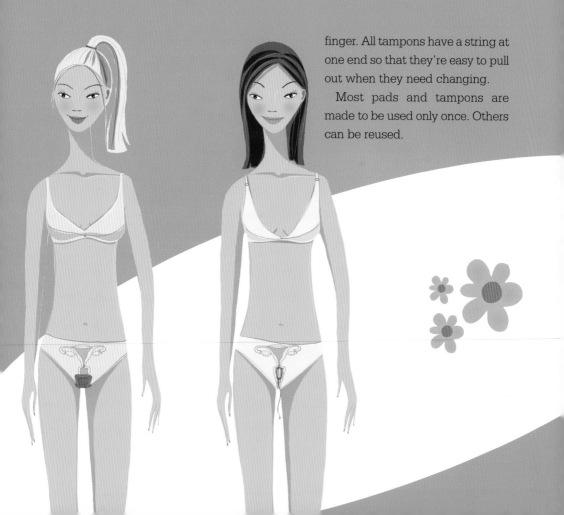

everything
a girl needs to know
about her
periods

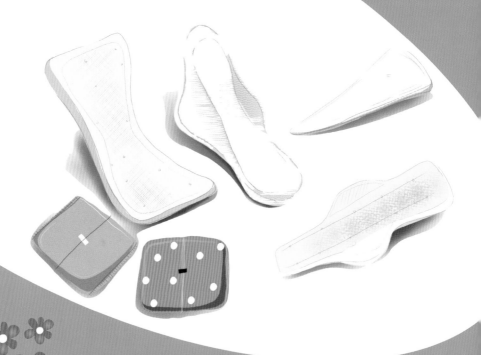

help!
how do I use a pad?

Pads usually come in three sizes: a panty liner, regular, or super. Use the larger sizes when you bleed more heavily or at night.

Pads are easy to put on. You just stick them onto your panties lengthwise. The adhesive on the bottom of the pad will hold it in place. Some pads have flaps or "wings" on the sides that will help keep blood from leaking into your panties.

You can tell just by looking when a pad needs changing. It's a good idea to check every couple of hours to see if you need a new one. When you're ready to discard the old pad, put it in a bag and place the bag in a disposal unit in a public toilet or in the garbage at home. You can't flush a pad down the toilet.

Pads are slightly bulky to wear and carry around. Shop around and try different products until you find the kind that best suits you—not all are created equal! You may want to store a few in your locker just in case you need an extra one when you're in school.

about pads

You can't wear them when swimming. You may want to postpone swimming on your heaviest days or wear a tampon when in the pool.

help!

how do I use a tampon?

Tampons also come in three sizes: mini or slender, regular, and super. Mini or slender tampons are usually best to use when you first start having periods.

Tampons have a number of advantages:

- No one knows you're using them, even when you're wearing a bikini.
- You can wear them when you go swimming.
- You can carry a spare in your jeans pocket.

But tampons are a little more complicated to use than a pad. Here are the details of how to put a tampon into your vagina.

relax and take your time

The key to putting in a tampon easily is to relax. Read the instructions on this page and on the box carefully. As you insert the tampon, breathe regularly and deeply, and take your time. You will get better at this with a little practice.

your step-by-step guide

one Wash your hands and unwrap the tampon. Crouch with your knees apart or stand with one foot on the toilet seat or bath. Hold the tube or tampon (if it's not in a tube) between the thumb and middle finger of one hand. Make sure the string is uncoiled and hanging down.

two With your other hand, spread apart the skin around the vagina. Place the end of the outer tube (or tampon) inside your vagina.

three If using a tube, push the bottom of the small tube up inside the larger one to slide the tampon in. Remove the tubes and put them in the garbage.

four If there are no tubes, put your middle finger on the base of the tampon and push it gently up toward your back. Stop when the length of your finger is inside your body.

five Make sure that the string of the tampon hangs outside your body between the outer labia. Wash your hands again.

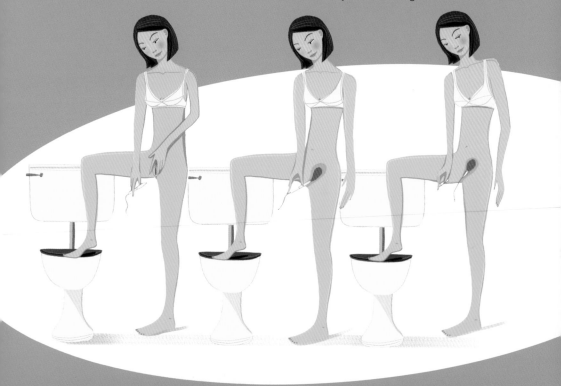

help!

w h a t   c a n   I   d o   t o   r e l i e v e   c r a m p s ?

Pampering yourself can help you get back on track on those days when your period (or premenstrual discomfort) leaves you feeling tired and crampy. Cramps are a pretty common occurrence during the menstrual cycle and they can happen at different times for different girls. We have mentioned at various times throughout the book what you can do to relieve those symptoms, but following are some more tips for getting additional help.

A long soak in a hot bath can relax your muscles and ease backache and cramp pain.

one Run a bath, turn the lights low, and have a warm towel and a robe ready when you get out.

two Use gentle bath soaps with skin softeners to moisturize your skin. Avoid bath salts: they can irritate sensitive skin.

three Try adding a few drops of essential oils to the bath water. The oils—made from plant extracts—are reported to help many people feel better. And they smell nice, too.

four Pat you skin dry after the bath rather than rubbing vigorously. Your skin may feel extra sensitive during your period.

Use common sense when trying oils for the first time. They can be of great benefit, but the following tips should be heeded:

• Never take any oils internally without first talking to a qualified health-care professional.

• Do not apply undiluted essential oils directly onto the skin. Try a skin patch test first before using an oil you've never used before. To do the skin test, place a small amount of the diluted essential oil on the inside of your elbow and apply a bandage (you can dilute by putting a drop or two of the essential oil into a few spoonfuls of olive, coconut, or grapeseed oil). Wait 24 hours to see if there is any form of reaction.

Lavender oil soothes the whole body and encourages a deep, restful sleep after your bath. Clary sage oil is said to act as a muscle relaxant and ease period pains. Marjoram oil is also reported to be good for relaxation, as well as black pepper, juniper, and rosemary.

top-to-toe tip: using oils

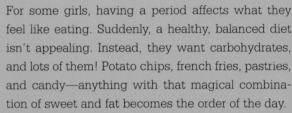

help!

what should I eat?

For some girls, having a period affects what they feel like eating. Suddenly, a healthy, balanced diet isn't appealing. Instead, they want carbohydrates, and lots of them! Potato chips, french fries, pastries, and candy—anything with that magical combination of sweet and fat becomes the order of the day.

Scientists believe that this desire for sugary, fatty food during the menstrual cycle has a physical explanation. The rise in progesterone causes a slump in certain other hormones, These hormones—serotonin and beta-endorphins—are linked to good moods. When their levels are low, we seek foods that will quickly increase them and make us feel happy again. Sugary carbohydrates are very good at doing this, but the downside is that the effects don't last long. That's why we're soon desperate for more of the same.

what to do about cravings

one You don't have to ignore them completely. Have a little of what you like.

two Try to eat plenty of complex carbohydrates. Fruit, potatoes, whole-wheat pasta, and bread all contain the right ingredients. They take longer than sugar to be absorbed by the body, so they create a more balanced mood.

help!

what if I'm a vegetarian?

The body needs iron to make red blood cells, which carry oxygen throughout the body. When you start having periods, you need more iron in your diet. This means that you have to be extra careful about eating the right foods, especially if you don't eat meat. Red meat is one of the richest sources of iron.

A vegetarian diet can be very healthy as long as it's well balanced. Most girls who aren't getting enough iron in their diet don't feel ill. Only a few become anemic, which makes them feel tired and dizzy. Even though you feel healthy, it's still important to eat the right things. Here are three rules to follow:

top-to-toe tip

If you're worried about your iron level, see a health-care provider. A blood test will show whether you have a problem.

If you don't eat meat, eat dark green vegetables like broccoli, spinach, watercress, or arugula every day.

Don't drink cola, or tea, or coffee with your meals. They contain tannins and caffeine, which stop your body from absorbing iron.

Always drink a glass of orange juice with meals. It's rich in vitamin C and helps the body use iron to keep you healthy.

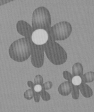

everything
a girl needs to know
about her
periods

f o o d   c h a r t

how you feel and look	*what you need*
Tired, prone to illness and zits	B vitamins
Worn out, dull hair	Foods rich in iron
Low energy and/or mood swings	Complex carbohydrates
General symptoms of PMS	Vitamin B6
Puffy face, hands, or feet; weight gain	Less salt and caffeine; more potassium
Tender breasts	Higher levels of essential fatty acids, vitamin E
Bloating, upset stomach	Less salt and sugar; more potassium-rich foods

what you should eat

Five servings of fruits and vegetables a day

Small portions of red meat; green leafy vegetables; beans

Whole grain foods; fruits and vegetables; raw carrots; fruit smoothies

Eggs; cheese; whole grains

Whole grains; bananas; nuts; potatoes; cauliflower

Tuna, salmon, cod; pumpkin seeds; walnuts

Bananas, cantaloupe, oranges; yogurt; cottage cheese; chicken; tuna

what to avoid

Refined sugar; pasta; frequent doses of caffeine

White bread; white sugar; candy; soda

Heavily processed foods with additives and preservatives

Salt and sugar; soda

Caffeine found in coffee, tea, cola; salty processed foods

Excessive salt like that found in chips, pretzels, popcorn; candy bars

Beans; vegetables like broccoli, cabbage, onions; cheese; ice cream

help!

what's an internal exam?

You probably won't need an internal examination until you are older. But now is as good a time as any to learn what happens when you do go for one.

When the time comes, you will need to make an appointment during a time when you are not having your period. During the exam, the doctor or nurse checks the health of your reproductive organs by looking through the opening of your vagina.

Some girls feel more comfortable having a woman doctor or nurse give an exam. But remember that men are trained in exactly the same way and will be just as sensitive to your feelings.

here's what's involved

one The doctor or nurse gives you a special gown to wear and asks you to remove your panties. Then you will be asked to lie on your back with your legs apart. If you don't feel comfortable, say so. It's part of the doctor or nurse's job to help you relax. This makes it easier to examine you.

two The doctor or nurse uses an instrument called a speculum to hold the vaginal walls apart. This makes it easier to see inside. You may feel the speculum inside you, and a slight pinch, but it doesn't hurt. Sometimes women complain that it feels cold. Using the speculum is one way the doctor or nurse checks the health of your internal organs.

three The doctor or nurse may put a finger inside your vagina and press gently on your stomach with the other hand. This is all a normal part of the exam. He or she is feeling your womb and ovaries to make sure that they're healthy and okay.

words, words, words, a glossary

There are many words about periods that you may not know yet. Some of them are medical terms used mainly by doctors and nurses. Others are words that are used by teachers, parents, and advice columnists. Here are a few of those words and what they mean.

cervix (SER-viks): the lower opening of the womb that leads into the vagina. The monthly flow of blood is released through the cervical opening.

endometrium (en-doh-MEET-ree-um): the lining of the uterus that is shed every month.

fallopian tubes (fuh-LOH-pee-uhn) tubes: hollow tubes that lie between the ovaries and the womb. Eggs travel through the fallopian tubes from the ovaries to the womb.

menarche (men-NAR-che): the medical term for a girl's first period.

menopause (MEN-o-paws): the time of life when a woman's periods stop, usually around the age of 50.

menstrual cycle (ment-STRUL-el) cycle: the time from the start of one period to the start of the next.

menstruation (ment-STRAY-shen): another word for period.

ovary (OH-vuhr-ee): one of two reproductive organs in women where eggs are produced.

ovulation (OH-vu-lay-shun): the release of an egg from the ovary into the womb.

period (PEER-e-ud): the monthly discharge of blood and other material from the womb through the vagina.

puberty (PU-burt-ee): the time during which a girl's body changes into a woman's body and a boy's body changes into a man's body.

uterus (YOOT-er-uhs) or womb: a hollow, pear-shaped organ in the pelvic area where a baby grows in a woman's body.

vagina (vuh-JY-nuh): a passageway made of skin, muscle, and fiber-like tissue that leads from the womb to the outside of a woman's body.

index

advice seeking 110–111, 117
age, first period 10

baths 37, 66, 130–131
beta-endorphins 96, 132
bleeding *see* menstrual flow
bloating 89, 93, 136–137
body changes, puberty 10–11, 20–21
body image 71
body temperature 68
boys 20
bras 72
breasts 10–11, 70–73, 89, 136–137

caffeine 72, 135, 136–137
calcium 101
carbohydrates 132–133, 136
cervix 14, 15, 23, 140
clitoris 25
color of menstrual flow 33
corpus luteum 68
cramps 34, 64, 66, 94, 105, 130–131
cravings 132–133
cultural issues 26–27

dental hygiene 95
diarrhea 106, 107
diet 79, 93, 106, 122, 132–137
discharge 11, 50, 58–59, 64, 81

disposal of sanitary pads 127
diuretics 103
duration
    menstrual cycle 56–57, 119
    menstrual flow 39, 47, 119

eating *see* diet
eggs 15, 22, 62
emotions 12–13, 82, 84, 88
endometrium 68, 140
energy levels 35, 85, 136–137
essential fatty acids 136
essential oils 130–131
estradiol 44
estrogen 18–19, 50, 74–75, 85, 96–97, 104
examinations, internal 24–25, 138–139
exercise 40–41, 94, 108–109, 122

fallopian tubes 14, 15, 22, 140
fertilization 15
first period 8–13, 26, 28–29
follicle-stimulating hormone (FSH)
    16, 18, 80
follicles 50
food chart 136–137

gonadotropin-releasing
    hormone (GnRH)
    16, 104

gums 95

hair 11, 136–137
headaches 89, 90–91, 105
heavy periods 42, 122–123
hormones 16, 18–19
hygiene 36, 95

inserting tampons 128–129
internal examinations 24–25, 138–139
iron 134–135, 136
irregular cycles 57, 119–121

journals 77, 112–115

labia 24–25
lifetime number of periods 118
low impact exercise 41, 108
luteinizing hormone (LH) 16, 18–19, 80

magnesium 101
medication 34, 66, 73, 90, 103
menarche 141
menopause 141
menstrual cycle 30–111, 119–121, 141
menstrual flow 32–33, 39, 42, 47
minerals 100–101
missed periods 121
moods 82, 84, 88, 136–137

napkins *see* sanitary pads

number of periods 118

odor 36
oils 130–131
ovaries 14, 15, 22, 141
ovulation 15, 16, 62–65, 141

pads *see* sanitary pads
pain relief 34, 35, 66, 72–73, 90, 103, 130–131
pampering yourself 99
perfumed sprays 37
period packs 61
period party 29
personal hygiene 36
pheromones 64
potassium 136
premenstrual symptoms 12–13, 87, 90–95, 97
premenstrual syndrome (PMS) 79, 87–89
progesterone 19, 68–69, 74–75, 80–81, 96–97
prostaglandins 34, 75
puberty 10, 20–25, 141
pubic hair 11

relaxation 99, 109

salt 90, 136–137
sanitary pads 124–127
serotonin 96, 132
signs, first period 10–13
sleeplessness 89, 92
smells 36, 62

stress reduction 98
stretching 41, 108
swimming 127, 128

talking 71, 79, 110–111
tampons 48–49, 124–125, 128–129
tearful outbursts 82
teeth 95
toxic shock syndrome (TSS) 48–49
tummy upsets 106, 136–137

uterus 14, 141

vagina 14, 15, 23, 24–25, 141
vegetarians 134–135
vitamins 100–101, 135, 136

water, drinking 66, 73, 93, 106
weight gain 136–137
womb 14, 15, 22–23

yoga 40, 99, 108

zits 92, 121, 136–137

First edition for North America published in 2003 exclusively
by Ronnie Sellers Productions, Inc.

No portion of this book may be reproduced,
stored in a retrieval system, or transmitted in any
form or by any means, mechanical, electronic, photocopying,
recording, or otherwise, without
written permission of the publisher.

Text and images © 2003 Axis Publishing Limited
All rights reserved

Conceived and created by Axis Publishing Limited
8c Accommodation Road, London NW11 8ED
Creative Director: Siân Keogh
Editorial Director: Brian Burns
Managing Editor: Conor Kilgallon
Production: Juliet Brown
Illustrator: Lucy Truman

Published by Ronnie Sellers Productions, Inc.
P.O. Box 81, Portland, Maine 04104
(800) 625–3386 toll free
(207) 772–6814 fax
www.rsvp.com
rsp@rsvp.com

ISBN: 1–56906–555–1; LOC: 2003106213

Printed in Thailand

10 9 8 7 6 5 4 3 2 1